Koccha
and Other Poems

KOCCHA

AND OTHER POEMS

ROBBIE SUGG

Day'sEye Press and Studios
PO Box 628
El Granada, CA 94018
info@dayseyepressandstudios.com
www.dayseyepressandstudios.com

ISBN: 978-0-9619714-5-8
Printed in the United States of America

Artwork by the author:
cover: Abbots Lagoon, 2011, ink/gouache
title page:: Beach Structure, 2011, lithograph
p. xv: Gene Pool, 2012, etching
p. 1: Scott Creek Structure, 2012, monotype
p. 29: Tamien (no. 2), 2012, monotype
p. 49: Cleveland Street, Chinatown, San José, 2012, etching
p. 51: Palomarin, 2011, lithograph

Photo of author by John Landry

For
Jim and Teri Sugg–
who brought me down to Earth

Contents

Author's Preface / ix
Introduction by Neeli Cherkovski / xi

I.   Koccha / 3

II.   San José Song / 30
       Haibun for Hungry Ghosts / 43
       Every Year Peregrine Falcons Nest
                    on Top of City Hall / 46

III.   Other Poems / 51

           Umbellularia Californica / 52
           Fraternity Row / 53
           Settlements / 56
           Redwood Suite / 57
           Substrate / 63
           木 / 66
           Observing Glen Park / 67
           I try to be so Buddhist / 69
           Architecture / 71
           From the Ground Up / 72
           Sometimes I Confront / 73
           San Francisco Invocation / 76
           All Night Making Images in San José / 77
           Weeds / 78
           Mele Ua o Hoʻoleʻa / 80
           Sustenance / 83
           The Green Unfurling / 84

Acknowledgments / 86
Author's Bio / 89

AUTHOR'S PREFACE

Much of this book sings of habitat, and the sense of self that ensues.

I was born in Berkeley, California, and spent my early childhood on the other side of the Berkeley Hills, on a commune that spanned acres of wild land on a semi-forested ridge. I vaguely remember the suburbs developing up to and around our property of 75-100 people, all living together. Halfway to adolescence, my immediate family moved down the ridge and into the suburban Diablo Valley.

Many of the poems owe themselves to the culture-shock-and-awe of being transplanted from a communal, semi-wild space, to a fenced in suburban space. Although this new residence was indeed suburban, our household was still a multi-family household, co-operative and communal, but on a much smaller scale than that of my early childhood. This non-traditional upbringing informs much of my sense of extended family, which is really a collective sense of self, (and this is closer to how humans have lived right up to the Industrial Revolution); it was also a fertile and contrasting backdrop with which to witness the wonder and weirdness of Californian-American culture.

Many of the poems were written upon moving to San José after spending an Autumn in and around Kyoto, Japan. Dissociated from my native place, and spending much of my undergraduate years studying the ravages and results of colonialism and industrialization, the poems emerged from my grappling with my sense of homeland as a white man in a globalized, post-colonial world. The plight of California's original inhabitants is of primary concern. This grappling was further complicated, as much of my extended family found itself grounded on the Big Island of Hawai'i, a place also overtaken by Anglo-American peoples within the last few centuries (but by no means completely).

These poems are links and planks in an endless attempt to bridge the divides between people in conflict and cohabitation with one another; by extension, they seek to heal the greatest divide of our time: that of the human-being, and the land from which it lives.

Robbie Sugg
2014

Reading Robbie Sugg

There is something exciting about reading a poet who is at the beginning of the long trek as a writer, especially when the poet has an innate ability to go for the poem as a complete experience. In his first collection, Robbie Sugg, trained as a visual artist at San Jose State University, turns to the page, inscribes his feelings, deepening our understanding of man in the world. It is for me, a poet of 68 years, a reminder of the continuity of the poem, "our poem", the one we listen for in the wind, in the trees, in the branches of the trees, in the birds circling the trees, in the shadows of a damp winter's morning, in the arid tones of a mid-afternoon in the summer.

Whenever I read another poet, a young one or an elder, I am rarely without a sense of wonder at what the mind can accomplish. "This person is doing something important, something that may survive his or her own time, and be of use in a future time." With this book, Sugg has the opportunity to be part of an old tradition. He has chosen well. His words ring with the authority of a person not yet thirty years of age, who is still deepening a poetic understanding, poised to move on into the refinement of his true nature.

Robbie Sugg is, indeed, young, but there are words in Koccha and Other Poems that reach far back in time. The collection begins, "KOCCHA, the word for house or home in the language of the Miwok people." This bit of information sets the tone for an exploration into deep history, both personal and land-driven. Sugg continues, "Hill, oak savannah, Umbellularia bay laurel, buckeye, sagebrush, chaparral, rolling down .. ." It all points to his place of birth, and to what he calls "Cleft of hills".

Sugg understands that the poem is what informs. The poet will stand in a state of awe as the world unfolds, as nature reveals: ". . . both sides of this culverted river that we are what separates us." His invocation of the native peoples of California, and his own identification with Scandinavian descent, is a risky business. He pulls it off. The sense is almost grandiose — he saves it through his devotion to the lyrical side of poetry. Like a bard just setting-out, Sugg is comfortable being transformed by the land around him, choosing the Greater San Francisco Bay Area's Mount Diablo for both ascent and descent — a natural monolith from an era before humans — the space that allowed his language to grow and prosper. As such, he appears well-anchored in "place", drawn to it naturally.

Long ago, the California poet Robinson Jeffers lifted myths out of the land, one ear to the rhythms of the coast and of the coast range, and one to the stories of early settlers who played out oftentimes tragic dramas against the rugged terrain where they had settled. Sugg has dug into the mythology of the land, but it is always a light touch, as if he was well aware of being "at the beginning" as a new traveler. This is where the strength of his poems lies. His line breaks are well ordained, as if he had a long history in the craft, and he knows how to conserve energy, making it easy for a reader to enter an unfolding vision. We are led to wonder what is it that makes for a native Californian? Where should one find a true poetic root from which to grow and thrive? It is quite unique how the poet deals with this issue:

For Earth carves its own body
    with its own tectonic
    body, unconscious of
    its consciousness

He has gone for the universal, embraced the planet, a true trope of the poet, and he does so with artistry. Further, he nails it down with a signature that brings our language right into the center of things. This is very much in line with the post-modern trend to write on writing. In Sugg's, however, there is a more traditional note — he insists on looping language around the framework of our experience as part of the human family, borders aside.

Every space between
     letter or breath of syntax
        is an ecology.
     Ancestry is poised on the tip
       of every sentence.

While not particularly lyrical, these are memorable lines. The lyrical side of the poet is ample throughout the book. Many of the lines have a Zen-like appreciation for the "tone" of the landscape:

Ever-present shifting
hue of Oak savannah
Green Winter
fades into dry hibernation
of Summer, day
by day by day

Sugg's writing is as rich as the illustrations he includes, all from his own hand. From abstraction to hard fact, from the seen to the unseen, the words are enhanced. This is a poet to be read and appreciated.

Neeli Cherkovski

— author of *Whitman's Wild Children* and volumes of poetry *Elegy for Bob Kaufman, From the Canyon Outward, Manila Poems,* and *Spent Shadow.*

I

Koccha

Koccha:

the word for house
or home in the language
of the Miwok People of
Northern Central California's
Sierra Nevada Foothills across
Central Valley Delta Plain through
Mount Diablo country out
crossing San Francisco Bay
through Mount Tamalpais' Coast Ranges
to the Pacific Ocean at what is
now called Point Reyes.

Saclán

was the name
        of the place –

A village defined
        by a territory
        of common ground

Hills, oak savannah,
        Umbellularia bay laurel, buckeye,
        sagebrush, chaparral rolling
        down

        Walnut Creek:
        "Arroyo de los Nueces
            y los Bolbones"
        was the blurred division.

        These people.
                Those people.

The plants of the sun-facing slope.
      The plants of the shaded slope.

Clefts of hills
      Summer blackberries
            Autumn acorns

      Half year dry
            Half year wet

Two-faced Earth
      both sides of this culverted
      river that we are
          what separates us

         ·
         ·
         ·

The accretion of memory
      as tectonic boundaries churn
            into Coast Ranges.

Ancient eruptions of new
      moments built up
            and eroded to the faulted
                  bedrock of epiphany.

A culmination of migrations and
      genetic processes of
            love after manifest
                destiny.

Chasing technologies and visions
        out West
Migratory parents in communes, suburbs, islands
Ancestors in the soils of
        Virginia, Carolina,
        Tennessee, New York,
        Illinois, Wisconsin,
        shores of Great Lakes.

Anishinaabe Bodéwadmi
Othaakilwaki Meskwaki
Tsalagi and *Seneca* lands
        places where the names are long and
        language lingers on tongues
        every syllable a story:
                Onöndowága', Tanasi, Wasioto,
                Jibaigan, Masu-kinoja, Shikaakwa

Every gene is a tap of the tongue
in the telling of spoken or unspoken histories,
        whole trails of them crossing continents
        like elk paths through dry grass or
        tangled strands of hair
        withering in the sun
        on the back of a turtle.

          .
          .
          .

The source
of this body's
instructions:

The cusp of Scandinavia–
        Islands, mounds,
        hammers, boats,
        petroglyphs, runes . . .

Genes carved into stones erected in lowlands
        below the melting millennia of glaciers:
        water places, bog and river places, lakes, wetlands
        where rains end their stampede to the facing
                        sea–

and the tendency of lowland Germanic
language is proliferation
        of synonyms for water
        its flows and forms:

                river, stream, creek,
                brook, drainage, slough...

For Earth carves its own body
      with its own tectonic
      body, unconscious of
      its consciousness.

"Tectonic"
as from the Greek: *tekton*
      "carpenter" or "builder"

Every space between
      letter or breath of syntax
         is an ecology.
      Ancestry is poised on the tip
         of every sentence.

                ·
                ·
                ·

At Lime Ridge
　　the rock is chalkier and whiter
　　than my own skin, all this calcium
　　the dust people of oceans

　　primordial soup settling
　　accumulating lithifying billions
　　of years gravitating, subducting,
　　striking, slipping, rising to
　　the surface

　　　　Creation stories
　　　　have consequences.

Even Coyote came
upon a raft
of tules and split sticks

It was all ocean
and islands, migrations
go deep

The land itself is pushed
elsewhere, this place was
assembled as a fringe

and this identity is offset
by a hemisphere
or two

I can't help when the myth
catches me by the toe
and pulls me under

bundles of bone, tooth
shell and dust, boats
and bulrushes are an old story.

That mountain
keeps growing taller
and taller

The higher you climb
the older
it is.

Our feet carry us to the top
of Mount Diablo, with all their
meat and bone, flashes of synapse
and sinew through chaparral
sandstone lip and skull
to the shoulders south
of her apex unfolding
like lotus in the cling
of Juniper.

A chewed up outcrop of
millions of years
of birthing and dying
protozoa fog of
skeletons mist down
compact into ground
pulled under and
pushed up
        here–

They say it was on this
uplifted strata that *Molluk*:
"Old Condor Man"
would perch to rest.

We climbed to the top and I'm somehow
giving a Japanese lesson looking out
over everything I've come to know
like the contour of this
yet short life.

O Molluk, did you see language
bubbling up along the seams of the Pacific Plate
did syllables steam from the fissures?

His father, Coyote,
created human in the image
of a cosmic joke
improvised and haphazard
          half-hazard.

A mere accident
of eyes looking out at
eyes looking in–

blood and tissue
cones and rods

planted feathers
pigments in skins

The walnut grove
at Shadelands Ranch:
500 acres bought
with Midwest money

Even the old Californio
elite fell on hard times
from time to time
ranchos can be a burden.

Ygnacio Valley Road was the way to work
through Heather Farms where
Ygnacio's house sat on land granted
to mothers in the *Pueblo, San José.*

They ran the deer out with cows
that they grew for their hides and tallow
leaving the carcass to rot
and they were surprised
that they were having trouble

with the Miwok
who in the absence of elk and deer
hunted the Mexican
cows for which these
grasses were planted.

Labored breath climbing the hill
where oak trees tie themselves in
knots, binding a hushed cacophony

of grass, the clamor
of wind in the ear

to see the basin of this genesis
from the hills above

what they called it then

    SACLÁN – VOLVON – CHUPCAN

this place that witnessed its people
    plagued and cloistered
    over the hills and across
    that turbid estuary.

    •
    •
    •

I caught a train to Oakland
spent the night and morning before
driving from Telegraph, Macarthur

and the 24 through tunnel
and hills of my birth, passing through
the spiraling route, through valley

around Mount Diablo, front to
back Marsh Creek Canyon
to the grinding holes at Volvón,

the deepest carved in sandstone
fed thousands, now swallowed
by Poison Oak, its numerous forms:

sapling, cascading vine
bush, tree, growing
in leaves of three

glossed with an infamous
oil, seductive red,
deciduous virulence

this escarpment beneath
the Blue Oak trees.

After C. Hart Merriam
as told at Ta´lasa´na,
Tuolumne Foothills

Loo'loo'e White-footed mouse
worked hard to get Fire
for the Foothill People.

White-footed mouse stole it
from the Valley People. To do this,
he first had to put them to sleep
with his Elderberry Flute.

Once his music had lulled them to sleep,
he snatched Fire and ran.
When the Valley People
and their chief, Eagle, awoke
they were pissed.

Humunya Hummingbird
had already worked so hard
to steal Fire for the Valley people
So they sent the Hail Storm
and the Thunder Shower
to get Fire back.

When Hail-Storm and Thunder-Shower
caught up with him,
Loo'loo'e White-footed mouse freaked–
he threw one ember in the water
and hid one in the *'unu,* the Buckeye Tree.

Hail-Storm and Thunder-Shower
told *Loo'loo'e* to cough the fire up
but *Loo'loo'e* had nothing

So Hail-Storm and Thunder-Shower went home
and *Loo'loo'e* snatched Fire out of the Buckeye Tree
and safely hid it inside his Elderberry Flute.

He took Fire to the Roundhouse of the Foothill People
and he placed it in the center of the Roundhouse,
and now the Foothill People could cook,
and stay warm around Fire

And then *Ossa'le* Coyote comes in
and he heaps a load of deer intestines on the fire
covering it up, nearly putting the whole thing out!

From then on, the People
changed Coyote's name from *Ossa'le*
to *Kat'wah* – "greedy"

And the People began to get cold
and only the People in the center of the Roundhouse
could talk as they could before

The People on the outsides of the Roundhouse
got so cold their teeth chattered,
and they could not talk plainly.

So the People separated into four groups
on the four sides of the Roundhouse:
The North People, the South People
The East People, and the West People

They all began to speak differently
from each other, and they all spoke differently
from the Middle People–

and this is how the People split up
into different languages and groups

They were driven apart
by the selfishness
of Coyote.

.
.
.

They would have us believe that ancestry
        dictates who we are, marriages or atrocities
        committed without the consent
        of descendents.

Or that DNA determines
        where we come from
        when the lay of this Land is threaded
        through my hips, my footsteps know
        where they stand.

I trace the contour every day
        and they will often tell me

I am not an Indian

        My hair is not black or brown
        My hair is Scandinavian
        My language is Germanic
        My writing is Roman
        My skull was forged in Europe
            with my limbs, my ribcage

My ancestors never stepped foot
in a Mission, never
smallpox, not that
I know of

My ethnicity, my genes, my
strange culture arrived late, not that
long ago
here, there were shellmounds
houses of tule, made from the Bay
        that wet-land of
billions of birds
        the Pacific Flyway flowing
                millions of years
abalone, fishing nets, adobe decaying
        towns, railroads threatening to
        sink down, abandoned houses
beds and linens
        eaten by mudflats
                and sloughs.

every August we would eat the blackberries
straight from the bramble, hot from the sun
all the kids' faces stained red-purple
for days and days pretending
they were tattoos, not one scolding
eye from any parent,

> and I find grass seed buried
> in my hair, the itch of burrs
> in my socks, my feet would be
> calloused and bare, shuffling through
> split cones and fallen acorns
> combing the dry grass
> hair of the hill.

I am not an Indian,

> but I hear them in whistling bone fog
> steaming off the ocean, over the
> Mountains, settling down in
> round houses, telling stories
> in the soil, weeping the floodless
> Coyote Creek.

my spine is a fault zone
my hair is manzanita
my lungs are oak
my heart is a grassland.

There is a trail crossing at Oak Grove Road
behind Graymont Circle, along Contra Costa Canal
     where the Concord Fault begins to couple
     the thrust fault
     of Mount Diablo.

It takes you through the stripped and malled
     ghosts of walnut orchards, riparia, a
     boned and shellmounded basin
          of subdivisions now called
          "Ygnacio", "Diablo Valley"
          and enters the hill country
            at Lime Ridge.

Cuts through this dissolution
     of Mexican land grants,
     old ranchos, crying rust,
     cattle gates,

          a forest of bedrooms
          and real estate steaming
          a dim constant roar.

the baking scent of wind
in fennel, sticky quaking
        grass

seeds, unnamed flowers,
the guttural tinnitus of red-wing
blackbird calls flaring from thickets

pierce the ears
and settle somewhere
behind the sternum,

burrowing a nest
in a heart of tules beating grasshoppers
with every step.

Can't count all the cars that drive over Lime Ridge
        every day– Ygnacio Valley Road is
        a constant suburban roar that buckles
        under the weight of heavy rains that came
        after the pierce and split of
        Summer Heat on the Concord Fault.

Four years spent crossing Lime Ridge
        by car, always wondering
        how to get to Lime Ridge.

        Four wet seasons.
           Four dry seasons.

Ever-present shifting
hue of Oak savannah
Green Winter

fade into dry hibernation
of Summer, day
by day by day

before eyes at sunrise
sunset, over and
back again, straddling

that ridge suspended between
two valleys, the reaches of

two fault lines, the pushed up shin
and ankle of
Mount Diablo

"Tuyshtak"
as neighboring Muwekma would call it
"Of The Day"
The navel of creation spirals out
unleashing dust
limestone
grass
seed

There was a willow thicket once
on the small river now called *Walnut Creek*
where a city named *Concord* now stands
once called *Chupcan* by the People.

When the Spanish tried
to round them up, a few of them
ran unseen into the thicket
which the Spanish called

El Monte del Diablo
"The thicket of the devil"
Then it became Mexico.
Then the Anglos came.

And they spoke Anglish
where "Monte" sounds like
"mountain" and that is how
Mount Diablo was named.

A linguistic mishap
and my location on this Earth
is tethered to It.

I only know where I am
when I know how far
in which direction I must walk
to reach that Mountain.

I belong to that Mountain.
She determines where I am
where I will go
where I will stay.

When I die, my ash will sift
through Her juniper
and gray pine.

I can only hope
that we will all hear
the original names for everything

of this place from the throat
of Old-Man Coyote Himself.

II

SAN JOSÉ SONG

El Pueblo de San José de Guadalupe de Támien
El Pueblo San José of the Weeping Señora
El Pueblo San José of the Southern Bay
El Pueblo San José of the Six Mountains
El Pueblo San José of the Ignored Rivers
El Pueblo San José of the Swollen Passage
El Pueblo San José of the Swirl of Regions
El Pueblo San José of Railroad Hegemony
El Pueblo San José of the Rapid Expanse
El Pueblo San José of Endless Subdivision
El Pueblo San José of the Salt-choked Slough
El Pueblo San José of the Pin-holed Rotunda
El Pueblo San José of the Festering Obelisk
El Pueblo San José of Electrical Exodus
El Pueblo San José of Destitute Affluence
El Pueblo San José of Culverted Mind
El Pueblo San José of the Delusioned Palm
El Pueblo San José between *Devil* and *Sacred Cross*
El Pueblo San José of Scattered Pacific Light

Hand-planted
redwood and fan palm
ascends the sky side
            by side.

Between the rivers
Guadalupe and Coyote
        the rains descend Winter,
                here–
                where floodplain once covered
                this soil in the skin and silt
                runoff of Diablo Range and
                Santa Cruz Mountains.

Where their hips wore aprons of madrone
            laurel, oak, manzanita
            flaring up from decaying
            quicksilver mines of memory.

This alluvial plain alone
        with its marshes in the vulva
        of San Francisco Bay has
        fed millions with its seeds
        and deer and abalone.

How many shellmounds have I slept upon?
        Lithifications of genealogies,
        burials of sunlight?

What uprooted creature is this roof?
        A whole sea of them
            suspended between
            the spines of fault zones.

They came howling silent
across the low river at high tide
over willows, trembling the *papal* with wind
blowing from dry Diablo Range.

"*Papal*" as spoken by the Tamien people or
"cottonwood" as we say.

They sift through various plants – sages and coyote bush –
      through nostril, felt brain tissue electrified
    as cottonwood is electrified.
        Subtle bodies easily touch
        subtle bodies, they knock at their temple
        gates like a flood.

        Though the levee
    has no doors, sycamores will gather
        on either side.

Passing through the heart
of town, the swollen
Guadalupe River

Simply breathing this
wet air, I am stoned
beyond description

Valley Oaks I never
noticed on the median
under the 280 overpass

The old pueblo
coughs up shards of China,
bricks, bowls and bottles

Guan Yin was bald and brown-skinned
wrapped in a Navajo blanket
at the crossroads

of San Fernando
and Market Street
This year the late rains

Winter came with Spring
the creeks heavy with seep
and persistent cherry blossoms

Funny they never
named Coyote Creek
after a saint.

El Camino changed course
to accommodate squares while
the river abides its course

Floodbanks altered
soil compacted for houses
and that flow remains

Passing through the heart
of town, the swollen
Guadalupe River

.

.

.

The condominiums on Guadalupe River
appeared as verandas of Kyoto Summer
on the river, Kamo, weeping willows, herons and all–
              the differences between the two:

              The *Kamo* River has no tules
              The *Kamo* River has no levee
                         One river is a virgin,
                         the other river, a duck.

              The similarities:
Both rivers dammed.
Both located in wide alluvial valleys
surrounded by mountains on three sides.

Both now hold a vast white collar industry
of information and communications technology.

Both once held a great population of people
who thrived so abundantly off of the existing
ecosystem that the birds and the wind
did all of their planting for them–

         but one agriculture replaces another:

One place, rice came.   The other, wheat.
         Almost exactly the same latitude.

Coincidentally enough, these ancient people
         and the Japanese people have the same word
              for rain.

日本町

Nihon-machi is Japantown
in Mother Tongue.

Spoken language binds itself
to the grit of sidewalks –
lichen to sandstone.

Detritus of tongue-sound or
   glottal stop in the gutter
   the poem filters through
   pine needles and shredded sycamore
   leaves lodged in the storm drain.

Source of consonant and
   vowel forged in the belly
   of an archipelago five-thousand miles
   across the Pacific

flows through the mouth
of the old hotel
the accumulation of this town

uttering the walls of flood control
and the confusion
of tortured sloughs.

Whorling in clouds of silt
        San Francisco Bay
        casts off its Winter as it tumbles
off the Sierras

Carrying a language out
        of the Golden Gate
        returning to that
        volcanic source
        from whence
        it came.

Kyoto, Japan and San José, California
    fall on almost the same latitude,
    but Kyoto's about as south as Los Angeles–
    figures: when outsiders think of Japan,
    they tend to think of Kyoto,
    and when outsiders think of California,
    they tend to think of Los Angeles.

The guidebooks rarely mention that San José
    was California's first civilian pueblo,
    or that Los Angeles followed San José
    as a model when the 1780s and 1790s
    rolled around: pobladores, cattle, disputes
    with mission lands, the works.

Yet the guidebooks usually mention how during
    the technology boom after the War,
    1950s, 1960s, San José followed
    Los Angeles as a model of suburban growth,
    emanating outward from the squares
    of the old pueblo.

        Old courthouse
        statues of dead presidents
        sleeping the homeless.

But Kyoto and San José have both been capitols
    at one time or another – Kyoto the third
    capital of Japan, had to get away from Nara
    (*Heijo*) with its bourgeoisie
    and the powerful, meddlesome Buddhist clergy.

Then a short stint in Nagaoka, on
Kamo River just downstream from Kyoto
where the river widens—
good for shipping they thought.
But the intermittent floods got nasty,
especially once the resulting diseases
moved into the imperial palace complex.

San José was the first capitol
     of the State of California, 1850 –1851
     but the first and second legislatures
     came to be known
     as "The Legislature of a Thousand Drinks",

          The booming dive bars
          pay day, after a long dry spell
          late torrential rain

and then the Guadalupe River swelled
     with a particularly severe flood,
     the likes of which the pueblo had not seen
     since 1797, when it had to move south
     from Taylor Street to where the center of town
     currently stands. As for the capitol,
     the water, mud, and liquor got to be too much,
     and after a quick stint up the Bay in Benicia,
     the fledgling government settled
     in Sacramento.

It colors outside
        the spectrum of rain

The wet season rolling in
        is a scatter of rusted leaves
        like where cow-paths meet
            driveways.

The silver gulp of Poverty Ridge
        seems to bend lip to its own ground:
            a prayer rug of *barrios*
            the intoxicated chant of car-sound
        scatter of language
            in valley strip malls
            Pacific Ocean turns
            in high fog

Haibun for Hungry Ghosts

Walking up and down Sixth Street, the temple roof
of Japantown rises like a wave out of the rust
of dead laundries, scorched brick, and quietude,
every so often the rattle of a wire fence in the attempt
to seal off a Chinatown called Heinlenville
leveled sixty years back – it was the largest Chinatown
south of San Francisco during its heyday but it didn't
take long for the boarding houses
to be boarded up and torn down.

The last remaining noodle house is empty,
the panels peeling, the walls dissolving
like the smoke of ghosts. Chain links can't contain
spirits – an invisible cloud hangs over Taylor Street,
"bad juju" they say, a strange condensation, even the
traffic's always dicey with a plethora
of easily avoided accidents.

> Faded signs, pounding
> jackhammers. A church, a temple
> a restaurant.

Come late Summer – time for the old *Da Jui*,
all but forgotten. In English – Festival
of the Hungry Ghosts:
hassled bachelors from Guangdong got some gigs
out here in *Gum San*,
doing the grunt work on Gold Mountain, picking
and planting, laying the roads and rails.

Law back then said women couldn't come–
"we got enough prostitutes." Guys always meant
to go back to China after they made their buck,
start a family to feed the spirit after they step
up to Heaven. But a lot of them
couldn't make the ticket home,
stayed and died a bachelor. No descendants
to leave out bowls of rice, stacked oranges, tsai,
a cup of wine or two to soothe the soul
when the veil gets thin. Now they got nothing
better to do than puff their smoke
up and down Taylor Street. Invisible gambling houses
shudder under the concrete.

> Temple bell sound sealed
> in gypsum and lime, late Spring–
> first cicada this year.

Now the Valley's Chinatown
is a spread out suburb where the rent is high.
People disperse. Spirits disperse.
Who could blame them?
When the 14th night
of the seventh lunar month rolls around,
I'd like to pay my respects to those
that came before, clap twice,
leave out some rice and a cup of wine
for the ones that never made it home.

Burn money in the streets.
Leave the bottle uncapped–
An empty red chair.

Every Year Peregrine Falcons Nest On Top of City Hall

The freeway ascent rising
      above city
      horizon

On the 7th floor
rolling car thunder projects
      incessantly upward

and swiftly passing students
      intermingling
      fractals of birds.

Above city sea
A throatful drone
cradled in mountains

A dusting of snow atop
two peaks if you look
      before the afternoon

Air still clear
after yesterday's rain
      how long will the grasses be green
      this year?

Redwoods barely rustle on the fringes –
straight tall anchored in
      to the alluvial hardness
      that washed off those mountains
        before the malls and onramps.

Descending Fifth Street, Japantown
Vietnamese Latino Chinese
Portuguese Pilipino Japanese
on couches on porches in
fog-filtered sun

the tangle of languages woven in
to the grid of metropolis
oriented with the faultline tilted
Northwest to Southeast.

San José is a Tower of Babel
laid flat on alluvium–
a grassland of roofs
a drained marshland of information technology
a savannah of roads and interchanges
conduits laid out
on the microchip of civilization.

The standing stone of city hall
cannot fathom the chug
of bicycle gears, bells and horns
of Mexican ice cream peddlers
the homeless shout
ruins of the broken hearted
Saint James Street.

Sixth, Seventh, Jackson, Taylor
Chinatown sold by the Great
Depression. Gutted and erased by 1949.
Now, a concrete lot, mostly abandoned,
slated for development, concrete eaten
by weeds and sun.

The global soup of this city
simmering in the cauldron of
a twice-named valley
    Santa Clara and *Silicon*
        and hundreds other
        names not made note of
        by the Spanish.

The volatile condensation
of worldviews in equilibrium,
cultures scatter and sink
into the aquifer of ancestry.

Where twelve miles from the nucleus
two tectonic boundaries push
those surrounding mountains upward
      one inch
      every year.

III

OTHER POEMS

UMBELLULARIA CALIFORNICA

What they call "Northern"
is actually as Central as the navel is
a braided web of drowned rivers
whose edges are not visible
on the maps of the state
whose motto is
      "Eureka!"

This *ria* at the Northern Center
of the California Bay Laurel range
once home to an unknowable profusion
of laurel species
back in the Miocene

     Nectandra
     Ocotea
     Persea
     Umbellularia

of these,
Umbellularia Californica is all that remains
of these Ancient Forests
found nowhere else
on planet Earth.

FRATERNITY ROW

Outside of this duplexed apartment
in the center of this big town, on either side
of the property line stand
three good, old trees:

A California Bay Laurel towering
whale of a canopy suspended of massive trunk
and dry leaf sun-baked incense
chaining my bicycle below the old
sagging porch.

A venerable Valley Oak,
Quercus lobata, "the lobed leaf"
capable of centuries, of sustaining
a human population
of hundreds of thousands before Spanish arrives,
now shading the back cabin
of a fraternity house.

Across the street, a redwood, human-planted
but particularly healthy, robust, immaculately
shaped like an older growth, on the edge
of the San José State University
business complex.

Except for the redwood, you don't see
too many of these trees,
lobed oak, California Bay,
in the center of such towns
anymore.

The old natives hug the outskirts
the foothills and open spaces, the face
of the wild space of your home-

   land

to hundred-thousand species
never sub-divided from their own
mosaical logic.

Nope, can't afford to own a modest
one-bedroom home in Saratoga,
Los Gatos, Mill Valley, Lamorinda going
for nine-hundred-ninety-nine-thousand

to live across the border from childhood,
to be in this place's indigenous state
you've got to stick to making
"a good living" as they say.

Unless you have lots of good friends
with communal inclinations, or
"fraternal" as we would say
in this case.

This hastily built cabin duplex seemed
so out of place in a town as old as this,
whose dominant species are
400,000 humans at its core
but sure enough the wise crows and the
hummingbird nest doesn't mind

the endless stream of car-sound
fraternity row chanting shots,
the scavengers and firetrucks and
constant foot traffic.

We offered a new home to the burgeoning
beehive in the lemon tree outside of
the front window, but the bees refused
to leave this place.

Hummingbirds refurbish the nest
crows and ravens return, the chickadees
can't stay away with their scampering
at the foot of this house.

The barking homeless
chirp of traffic lights
passage of birds, redwood
bay laurel, old valley oak.

SETTLEMENTS

Snow dust tint
              bald mountain tops
       Oaks congregate
             in gulches.
Cities creeping up
     her hips.

REDWOOD SUITE

In Santa Cruz Mountains
where there still stands
old growth redwood
he asked: "What's everyone looking at?"

What not to look at?

In San Francisco
you can see a tree older than Jesus
turned into a house.

San Francisco Bay–
metropolis built
on cycles of booms,
busts, and rushes

for gold or numbers in machines,
massive influx of cash straps
and cars and trains
that carry them

flooding marshlands with capital
separating sediments
translated into levels
of income, constant resettling

process driven by dollars
and change
as indicated by stock tickers
or seismographs or maps

charting liquidity
of soil that was once
debris of a flourishing
many years ago

resurrected and retro-
fitted for the second coming
of a cycle repeated many
times over and over

the striking of some vein
of another seventh heaven
center of the bohemian mandala
time bomb of hipsters

with the next edenic becoming
in the constant search
for the "est" of everything
in this culture of superlatives

Redwoods didn't plant themselves
in Redwood City, California—
it was coast scrub, mixed oak
woodland, and tidal flats.

Redwood City, California was named
for the redwoods that passed through it
drawn, quartered, and ported to build
the first neighborhood in San Francisco.

Train lines stick to old routes:
The old growth was cut short
by the White man and buried
by the Chinese man.

Where the homes rise like rice paddies
of terraced mothers and fathers
growing their babies high and dry
above our flat world

of taquerías and Chinese restaurants
salt ponds and industry, low highways,
train tracks, and remedial
marshland.

.
.
.

North Town, South Town,
East Town, West Town,
all quadrants of the socio-
economic color wheel.

Boundaries drawn
by bus routes where they
fade out into
real estate.

Are you an urban poet?
Are you a nature poet?

To get to the edge of the answer
you've got to take a long walk.

Redwood drinks fog before sunrise.
Tilted back, looking up
I can hardly hold back tears

Ancient wooden sea
burl after burl
the pinnate extension

threaded through spinal trunk
leaned bent over backwards with
the will to live onward and upward.

Redwood, you've stood two-thousand years
and all I have to offer is this
Mount Diablo heart.

.
.
.

SUBSTRATE

I close my eyes and see a tree
    growing in my esophagus
    the meaty bark, the branching capillaries
    lungs ebbing tiding ceaseless
        heart beat
        leaves drop
        feed roots.

What thoughts have they but space?

A cavern ribcage filled with rain
Past life future
        life

    what do we know?

        .
        .
        .

The center follows only the center
driven of its own accord.

Everything in the Universe is drawn
to Everything in the Universe.

The Mother says:
When left to its own devices
water flows only to where
it is needed.

The oceans would plunge into the heart
       of Earth's burning belly
         if basalt did not stand
         firm in its path.

If no gravity,
That belly
would not burn.

If no rock
no ocean

no water
no primordial soup
        origin of life
no single cell
        division in the force of
        some unfathomable devotion
        to split the helix of yearning
                and a burning liquefying lithifying
                hurling mass flares up
                among All Things:

        dust, river, vein

    tendon, juniper, tooth

        a trunk, a spine, a root

木

How to grow
     the self
     and eat light

The instructions are written
     in leaves
     in their green vein
        rivers
     blood vessel watersheds
     fanning out from the central
        trunk heart column
          breathe
        and flow

Lungs planted into the land
by water or gravity
     or forgetful squirrel

The Oak rustles at 3 AM
     carrying the weight of millennia
Free of a brain
     its silent mind
        flows in the grain

Meat body or
Wood body, we share
     the same breath.

Observing Glen Park

Clouds diffuse
over the canyon,
plank houses
      rise on stilts to meet
      the rice paper sky.

A commotion of birds,
talons in a nest of hair
clutching umbrella tighter
      feathered fearless stare
      of pigeons at my feet.

Forded the crosswalk
      incensed with exhaust
      carried on wet breeze to
         another lung.

Familiar smells of eucalyptus
        glimmer of rain in the air
              ocean wind
dust in the streets
        of the fog-eyed city
        bathed in gray milk of clouds
        painting the town monotonous.

A bench to sit on,
a sidewalk to lay the soles of my feet,
lines in the pavement to contemplate

through which insistent birds pluck
        invisible seeds
              that fell from creation
              now a pearl tossing
              in the belly.

I TRY TO BE SO BUDDHIST

about "things"
        "No attachment" attached
        to every attainment–
            All emptiness
            anyway.

But I can't help the attraction
        to it
        the Spirit of Objects
            as revealed by the hand
                long-gone.

Particles form, wood grows its self until
        some hand cuts it with
            vision or
            no vision
        joins it, nails it, carves,
        polishes surface, shines its
        iridescent nature, making a table
            a wall, a statue, a bowl could be similar
to
        the gravity that everything
        gravitates to.

The body of a Tibetan ewer made of
two human skulls joined at the brow
ridge from which the pouring teaches
        that the mind
        is egg-shaped.

I cannot separate myself from the notion
that consciousness is palpable.

A brain is three pounds and many miles
wound around itself, could be spread
across the length of the spine
of this fault line
        when Everything orbits
            Everything.

To float the river of ash
through the Milky Way
        Many look into the glow of screens
        for news or story when
                the oldest story is revealed
                when you find yourself looking
                    into stone.

ARCHITECTURE

I live in a concrete monolith
cells divided by
>> sheetrock plaster plateglass plastic
>>> pipeline blood vessels
>>> cars parked in the bowels
>> straight cut standing tall
>> a clocktower (no one reads)
>> to top off
>>> hotel consciousness.

Walking back from the library
>> cheap paint, brain colored
>> highlights, Winter Valley Oak
>>> branches, currents curling
>>> through leafless lung

Passing under naked canopy
>> cold wet air
>> biting my thin-boned hands

didn't notice my old friend
>> walking by.

From the Ground Up

Squirrels hold ground up September
acorns in cheeks like half-read poems.

An eye glints a sigh
with the subtle awareness

how withheld syntax can leach
the tannins of that
which is already known.

Sometimes I Confront

I

Library
　　　　books like firecrackers
in the brain.

Good, big windows
can see the Santa Cruz Mountains turning
　　　　in Pacific fog,
　　　　　　　　rolling over in their sleep
　　　　licked by Marine layer
　　　　this valley is many civilizations
　　　　come and
　　　　gone.

I've been circling the bay winding round
countless migratory pathways
　　　　in car
　　　　burn fuel, "hybrid" makes little
　　　　　　　　difference–
　　　　my bodhisattvas tend to spread themselves
　　　　　　　　out

City upon city
Planes descend into San Jose airport
    birds follow.

Mountainous trinities mark every home
    I've ever belonged to

        Tamalpais, Umunhum, Diablo
        Mauna Kea, Mauna Loa, Hualalai
        How many carbon cycles
          have they seen?

II

A world made from a Mother's flesh
    suck Her dry
    our ways are strange
    to the Void

It
doesn't care
about subprime mortgage
crisis economy crash black white
brown invisible president nation flag
birth death oblivion creation
right wrong America
is but a name
no more than
a name.

The land speaks its self.

Peak oil's getting me down again.
    In some years' time our kids will
    again understand the importance
    of a river.

Why to worry when the rains
    remain in the sky in January

Rediscover fire
how long until the Internet
    is a myth?

San Francisco Invocation

O Goddess San Francisco
who are vastly loved
creatively immense, dense

besieged by her own wealth
and the confluence of a happenstance
most fortunate location

"Gold Mountain"
may your prosperity
not cripple you,

your triangular shadows, piercing
light on carefully carved wood

fraying the seams
of public and private

false fronted, high ceilinged
rectangular recessed neatly

climbing the face
of hubris and a heap
of horses at the bottom
of these hills

may cassava and mango continue
to overflow the awnings
of 16th Street.

ALL NIGHT MAKING IMAGES IN SAN JOSÉ

I drink beer in the cold light
afterglow of silkscreen meltdown
reading his poems and photographs.

The sycamores of San José
spew their dust, scented air
of baking grass.

Could taste the texture
of reality, the warp and the
weave of atoms like canvas

soaked in oil
pigment under nails
overslept dreams forgotten.

WEEDS

Last night I saw dreams of Japan,
old housemates, and zombie breakouts
or the other night when I dreamt
he was leaving six months or that
I was off to cross the Pacific
without having packed, no money
not even a dictionary.

After death, the Coast Miwok
would cross the Ocean to the Village
of the Dead. Sometimes they come
back at night to dance in the round-
house. San Francisco Chronicle
reports that biologists stationed
on Farallon Islands, twenty-seven miles
off-shore, simultaneously experience
the same palpitating nightmare for weeks:

"wild dogs and squawking children
bombard the island, smashing eggs,
trampling nests, burrows and dens.
Mothers abandon their young.
Babies are crushed."

They moved in again after I told them
to mail their keys to the landlord.
I found a plane ticket for Osaka
no lover coming, just dead hands
reaching through the window.

Couldn't find him the next
morning until I found him
sleeping on the daybed
silent as a painting.

He's elsewhere with averted eyes
and I'm still trying to remember
if I'm due somewhere while he
watches his toast toasting with
the butter ready on the knife,
one leg outstretched like mudra.

He rustles boxes of blotted morning
light, the patience of the approaching
afternoon emulates the weeding
of each little sadness fragile
as a newborn root.

Mele Ua o Hoʻoleʻa
Song of the Rains of Hoʻoleʻa

I

Ua kea – "white rain", mist
tumbles in great sheets
weightless on tradewinds
At the periphery, vision bends
tracing that wide base line, elevation zero
changes over years, curves
at the edge of the eye.
Curved as any swollen belly
huge above this bowl of orchard
where it seems to drop off
to the sea of her face.
Seeing through eyes of leaves or
speaking in tongues of bark
the crickets chirped experimental
as electric sound.
Spirits ring this Ocean
funneled up through
the basalt navel
birthing outward.

II

Ua lani pili –
"rain where the heavens stick to the Earth"
a torrential rain that appears suddenly,
and pours intensely for days
Mist obscures familiar music
where green ridges are suspended
whether human or Mother Earth planted
on the borderlands of watersheds
funneling the extensions of great clouds
reverse delta'd to a single stream
of consciousness gulched and waterfallen
at the meeting of land and sea
this *lokuloku*
flooding the mysteries of emotion
penetrating this shell of human habitation
tears drip through ceiling
wall and cross beam
downpour saturated ground
spilled over and bawling down,
stripping the earth
from the posts of this house
soon you'll know what it is
to be possessed by this water.

III

The thicket encroaches the feet
of this bungalow, air heavy
with what is called
ua kilikili, "little rain"
a kind of mist or drizzle
that plants drink
through the skin
of their leaves
Some-one-thing unfathomable
vibrates here, you cannot
grasp it. It
grasps you, caught
between the thighs of it.
My skin crawls as a baby does
caressing with eye and pulse.
The piercing drone of the soil
steams its fragrance
The tiniest droplets
find their way in –
the dank smell.
The earth grows
red, utterly
engorged.

SUSTENANCE

I spent the day wandering
in a series of still lives
ate light for breakfast,
lunch, and dinner
gathered my senses
like seashells.

Having leads to
chores in the house-
keeping of balance.
Tomorrow:
wash clothes
visit post office
procure "healthcare"
note that insurance is not assurance
of the capital necessary
in the act of self-
preservation.

Biggest achievement this week:
Remembering how
to breathe.

THE GREEN UNFURLING

of leaf
single shoot straight up
pointed tip
unraveling birth, the devotion
of cells at work.

The opening and the
beckoning of penetration
by light – says I Ching
The receptive gives way
to the creative.

Offshoots, new beginnings
roots weave effortless thru
volcano soil.

Under the mac nut tree where we smoked last year
           wind in the bamboo and eucalyptus
The old bench droops lower than it did last spring
Wet with rain and fog of
              one thousand mornings.

To Hawaiians the god of rain
           is rain.
      Blue wet haze fade back
      mist down in sheets and swells
      dodging blankets of sun.

          Sink in
          feed roots
          become fruit.

Acknowledgments

I'd like to thank the editors of the following
journals and anthologies in which some of these poems
first appeared:

Diane Lee Moomey, **Day's Eye Press and Studios,**
for this volume;

Jake St. John and Colleen Keenan,
      Flying Fish and Elephant.
Kathryn Kulpa, *Newport Review.*
Christine & Dennis Richardson,
      Willow Glen Poetry Project.
Harry Lafnear,
  Shared Light and *No Ordinary Language.*
Vuong Quoc Vu,
  Caesura and *Perfume River Poetry Review.*
John Bonanni & Gemma Leghorn
   Cape Cod Poetry Review.
Steve Luttrell and Wayne Atherton,
      The Café Review.
Divya Dubey, *Earthen Lamp Journal.*
Raindog Armstrong, *Lummox.*
Mitchell Lafrance, *Eternal Breakfast.*

Heartfelt gratitude to my teachers:

Gale Antokal, Michele Birkenshaw, Robert Chiarito, Steve Durie, Donald Feasél, Jeff Hagerstrand, Charles McLeod, Leroy Parker, Patrick Surgalski, Tom Wills, Betty Wong

And deepest gratitude to the following for their support, guidance, and generosity:

Jesse Cabrera, Neeli Cherkovski, Richard Diebenkorn, Diane DiPrima, William Ericson, Agneta Falk, Karen and Richard Flittie, Allen Ginsberg, Pam and Dan Glassoff, Kina and Wailehua Grey, Dana Harris & Yori Seeger, Justine Highsmith, Jack Hirschman, Van Jackson-Weaver, Lakshmi Kerner, Joanne Kyger, John Landry, Hung Liu, Greg and Tania Manning, David Meltzer, Sarah Menefee, Ian Newan, Nathan Oliveira, Dave and Sherry Pettus, Tiffany Porten, Al Preciado, Shairy José Quimbo, Valerie Raps, Nanao Sakaki, Erica Shroeder, Gary Snyder, Jessica Sugg, Sweet Sanctum/ Virginia Barret, The Beauty Palace, Freddie Vega, Lew Welch, Eric Whittington, Zarina

Robbie Sugg studied painting, printmaking, papermaking, and Japanese language at San José State University. His artwork has appeared in galleries throughout the San Francisco Bay Area, as well as in New Bedford, Massachusetts, New York City, and Worcester, England. He plays the guzheng, a 22-stringed ancient Chinese zither. Presently, he lives with one foot on the Big Island of Hawai'i and the other on the shores of San Francisco Bay.

Made in the USA
Charleston, SC
03 March 2014